T0163592

Wake Up!

Advanced Praise

Relevant, real, and relatable. Relatable and really relevant. That's the kind of wisdom Janet Ellis provides, as she takes us on unexpected life excursions and gives us the opportunity to learn some of life's most important lessons alongside her.

-Jana Stanfield
Multi-Platinum Songwriter and
Everyday Philanthropist

Wake Up!

Break the Generational Cycle
and Be Yourself

JANET ELLIS

NEW YORK

LONDON • NASHVILLE • MELBOURNE • VANCOUVER

Wake Up!

Break the Generational Cycle and Be Yourself

© 2019 Janet Ellis

Published in New York, New York, by Morgan James Publishing in partnership with Difference Press. Morgan James is a trademark of Morgan James, LLC. www.MorganJamesPublishing.com

ISBN 9781642792980 paperback
ISBN 9781642792997 eBook
Library of Congress Control Number: 2018911714

Cover & Interior Design by:
Christopher Kirk
www.GFSstudio.com

Morgan James is a proud partner of Habitat for Humanity Peninsula and Greater Williamsburg. Partners in building since 2006.

Get involved today! Visit
MorganJamesPublishing.com/giving-back

Foreword

In the fall of 1995, I met and became close friends with Fred Rogers, the icon of children's television and one of our culture's secular saints. It was time of great inner pain for me, and from the first Fred tried to coax it out into the open. He called the pain my Furies. "Anything mentionable is manageable," he would say, or he would quote his good friend, the great Catholic writer Henri Nouwen, who said, "What is most personal is most universal." In other words, my anger, my sadness, my depression, my shame, was not something bad, but part of my humanity, and in fact, what I most shared with other members of my species.

A year after we met, Fred sent me Henri's latest book, The Inner Voice of Love: A Journey Through Anguish to Freedom. It was his diary of the time Henri spent recovering from an emotional breakdown. Fred told me that he thought it was one of his friend's finest books because "it was his most personal, which is often the most universal."

I am reminded of these things now after reading another book, this one by Janet Ellis. I wish Fred could have read it, too. He would be as grateful for it as I am. Janet, like Henri, has gently reminded us, by telling her own amazing story, what it truly means to be human, and that we are not bad because we suffer; we suffer because we are human.

But that primal pain is unnecessarily compounded. One of the greatest of all human afflictions, I believe, is not that existential suffering, but the isolation and shame we feel as we work so hard to conceal the often-messy truth of our insides from one another. Janet, like Henri and others in what I think it a growing human movement toward authenticity, invites us out into the light to tell the truth about our lives.

As Janet herself demonstrates, that brave truth-telling is not the end of the story. In many ways it is just the beginning. Much healing and authentic suffering needs to be done as we explore old wounds and give them the attention they deserve. But in that journey, the burden becomes gradually less heavy, and we are revealed to ourselves. We learn what we are truly put on this beautiful planet to do.

Janet was put here to help us heal. She is a minister, a life coach, and speaker, and now an author. This book is brave, generous and wise. It's not easy reading. She in fact dares you to read it, then to take up your truth and start down the road to healing. Please take her up on her dare. She has been down that road before you, and with these words, lights your way toward freedom.

Tim Madigan

Author of *I'm Proud of You: My Friendship with Fred Rogers*

Table of Contents

Introduction

There is a deep desire within each and every one of us – yes, each and every one of us! However, we don't all know it. Many of us will never know, and some of us have an awareness but will make a choice to numb that feeling in any way we can because it feels too big for us. Others of us take a look at our dream or need, and then once we have gone beyond our comfort zone, we stop.

Then, thankfully, there are those who have heard their call, and, no matter how they attempt to ignore it, they can't. These are the individuals who are so interested in doing whatever it takes to wake up further to their dream and do whatever it takes to get themselves there. They will not use as an excuse where they come from, how they have no money, how they were abused. No matter what situation could get in their way, nothing stops them from being who they are meant to be and shining their light.

How about you? Are you one of them? If so, this book is for you. In these pages is an opportunity for you to breathe and know that you are normal, you are not alone, and there is a way to get through the crap without giving up.

I dare you to read this book. I dare you to take a deep breath, take the time to go within and just get quiet. I dare you to ask yourself one question, maybe one of the most important questions you may ever ask yourself: What is mine to do? At this point if you get an answer – awesome. If you don't – awesome! Either way, if you are drawn to this book, you are ready and longing to find that answer and move forward on it finally.

Every day you make choices – perhaps as many as 650 decisions a day or more! These choices either take you closer to where you want to go or take you farther away. If we stop long enough to look within instead of looking for answers outside of ourselves, guidance on who we are and how we want to show up is the most important thing we could ever, ever have. Wanting what you want versus getting what you want is where we want to go.

If you walk around a bookstore, you can see books on how to get everything sitting right by books on how to live simply with less. There are books about how to lose weight next to books on how to be fat and happy! What I realize is that no one has the answers, no one knows anything; however, whether you believe you can have it all or that having it all is too cumbersome boils down to one thing and one thing only: it is all a state of mind.

> *"To know you have enough is to be rich beyond measure."*
> – Lao Tzu

In this book we will determine what your purpose is and why you are here – and you certainly are meant to be here, or you wouldn't be. This book offers practices, daily routines that give your life structure and help you cultivate the passion to show up every day as who you say you are.

Every one of us has room to improve. We at some point turned off of the path we were meant to be on and ended up getting caught up in life as we know it. We have lost ourselves, not intentionally, but that is just the way it is. But we are now at a point in our lives when we know there is more to live for and changes to be made to become present to all and everyone around us. It is no longer just "all about me"; it is about wanting to be so powerful that we have an effect for the better not only on ourselves but also on everyone around us. It is wanting to see others succeed instead of seeing things as competition; it is believing that life is meant to be lived in a way we never imagined before – and when we do, we create amazing experiences, knowing there is something so much bigger than ourselves in the world.

This book will assist you in waking up to who you are and what you want to be. It is also a personal share of where I came from, where I went in my life, how I knew I didn't want that life anymore and finally woke up and stepped into the person I wanted to be and the life I wanted to live. I share stories of experiences I have had that are deep and some that are miraculous, which I am constantly in awe of.

The biggest part of this whole process is the "doing it." If we did a piece of what we already knew, we would be kicking butt and not searching outside ourselves and looking for help to heal us; we would be in pretty good shape. What I want to share is that, as a human being, I needed help. I so wanted a gentle reminder and an accountable "kick in the ass" to get the doing it part done! There is nothing wrong with us, we are not "broken" or damaged, we may have just lost our way and are now wanting guidance to get back on course.

Support, being heard, and accountability are so important if we want to bring ourselves back to where and who we are truly meant to be. If you are ready to do the work, I am ready to be there with you and for you. You've got this, I know you do. I believe in you!

Chapter 1
You Are Normal!

"The most beautiful people I've known are those who have known trials, have known struggles, have known loss, and have found their way out of the depths."
– Elisabeth Kübler-Ross

There are times when you believe you know what you know and you really don't know that you don't know that you don't know! Great way to start, isn't it? What I mean is that we have a world of individuals who are all walking around clueless to who they are or what they're even doing here … they are so asleep and out of tune with the world that they really don't know that they don't know. Disconnected, numb, asleep – whatever terms you want to use, it is disheartening to witness this and yet I totally understand where they are coming from. It is a prison that we don't even know we're in – that used to be me!

We are so anxious about what is going to happen in the future that we don't enjoy the present, with the result being, we don't live in the present or the future. We end up living feeling like we're never going to die and then we die never having truly lived. We spend so much time living in our heads and believing what we have created there, so consumed with those stories, that our reality has become unreal and isn't even close to what our life truly is.

When you grow up in an abusive environment, so much energy and time are invested in staying one step ahead of the abuser, in that you make sure that everything at home is in its place and that nothing will trigger the abuser to set them off. You constantly feel as if you are walking on eggshells attempting to stay out of harm's way or are creating an environment that is quiet so as not to stir anything up. This creates intense habits that are ingrained in you for life.

Of course, you don't realize it at the time because all you are doing is staying in survival mode to protect yourself and your family and to make it as safe as possible. What ends up happening is all the behaviors you learned as a child that kept you safe and helped you survive are now still with you in your adult life. What then happens is that every relationship you have, be it with family, friends, or a romantic partner, is affected by these behaviors. Most of us have no idea that these behaviors come from our upbringing because they are so habitual and such a part of our nature that we really don't know that we don't know.

So you now are in a place where your outside world looks like utter chaos, family, friends, lovers are upset, frustrated, angry at you, and for the life of you, you have no idea why. When we feel stuck, depressed, angry, constantly hurt and we find we are saying things to loved ones we know hurt them, but we cannot stop or control it, we hurt others knowing it is wrong, get angry with ourselves, beat ourselves up, and feel absolutely miserable. The vicious cycle then begins again.

When I was six, witnessing abuse became my first memory. I was never physically abused; however, witnessing emotional, verbal, and mental abuse ended up creating an insecure, sensitive, and defensive dynamic that I lived in. I went along in life stuffing the feelings of pain, anger, and hurt, not realizing what I was doing because it was such an automatic, habitual behavior. It was such a part of me, it was who I was!

When I became a young adult, it had such an effect on me, I didn't even know the meaning of "healthy" relationships. I stayed so stuck in my old hurts that I didn't even know I could move into new, glorious experiences. As long as we continue to live in the behaviors we learned as children, we can end up stuck in the past forever, especially if ours has been an unhealthy environment. As children, we are totally dependent on others to keep us safe and to help teach us right from wrong. These others do the best they can with the skills they have, which they learned from their own parents. What their own childhood was like determines how they will be as parents.

We either choose to do things the same exact way we were taught, which is the norm because it is the habitual behavior we know, or we attempt to do the extreme opposite of what we were taught because we no longer want to have that particular dynamic in our lives. We do not always make the best decisions for ourselves because of the negative thoughts we carry in our mind and the fact that we believe what they tell us. When we continuously believe the negative thoughts that we have carried around with us our whole lives, we are working from that energy, and then we wonder why our outside world looks so negative and chaotic.

There are so many different ways that these behaviors can show up at work, in our relationships, in our lives. It is so easy to react to situations in everyday life from pure, raw emotion, as we see people do on a daily basis on the news: shootings in schools, suicides, families murdering each other, coworkers taking care of business by killing innocent people. All of these individuals are in so much pain and they do not know what to do with the energy they are carrying, so they release it in intense, dramatic, unhealthy dynamics that then create more hurt energy. *Hurt people hurt people.*

When I finally began to take a look at myself and what kind of thoughts I was having, it was shocking. I had no idea what to do with the way I was behaving; it seemed a losing battle. The pain was so deep and I was so wounded that I couldn't see past it to attempt to better myself and do something different with my life. I was a slow bloomer for sure; however, something within me was even deeper than the pain, and no matter what I did to hurt myself, I always heard this voice deep down inside of me telling me that I was here for a reason, that I was here to do something big, and that I needed to find someone to help me.

I searched (and am still searching to this day) for any healthy way to better myself and know that I am worth keeping around and am worthy to share who I am and what I stand for. Of course I didn't know what that was in the beginning, but with the inner nudge I kept getting and by connecting with individuals who came into my life who proved they wanted to help me and see me succeed, I have become the awesome person I have always wanted to be, inwardly and outwardly.

There are so many out in the world who know what I am talking about in regard to the feelings of knowing what we are doing isn't right but not having any freaking idea as to how to change ourselves or our behavior. The pain is what gets in the way. The wounded child who didn't get their needs met is always in the forefront, living your life for you, making decisions for you, reacting to situations for you. If you see yourself behaving in ways that you can't stand, yet can't seem to control, such as acting immature, being self-absorbed, playing the victim, and constantly blaming others about what occurs in your life, the thing about it is, in every situation that is showing up negatively or hurting you, you are the one and only person in every one of those situations no matter how many other people are involved – I know it sucks to realize that!

This can be very confusing sometimes, especially when we have been abused by someone in some form or fashion and it sounds like we are the ones being blamed for it. That is not the case at all. The only thing is, we play a part in all of it, and until we are willing to see that and take a look at the part we are playing, we will never be able to get past what is going on and help ourselves get healthy.

How do you talk to yourself, harshly or lovingly? How does harshness keep you from seeing the beauty of who you are and making the changes you want to see in your life? We often tell ourselves things that are so cruel we would never dream of saying them to someone else. Where did those thoughts begin, where did they come from, and how have we had them in us without knowing that they were there in the first place? Easy, we adopted everything that family, friends, teachers, parents, siblings, and anyone else who was in our life from early on shared with us. One of my biggest passions is to break the generational cycle from which we live our lives daily, not even knowing we are doing it because it is so habitual.

No matter where you are in life, no matter what you are doing, the biggest thing you need to know and get is that you are normal and there is absolutely nothing wrong with you. Although our behavior may not be up to par, the blessing is that we get to change it and become who we are truly meant to be: a healthy, loving, compassionate individual who wants to make a difference in the world and leave a magnificent legacy of love.

Chapter 2
We Are the Same

"It's never too late to be what you were meant to be."
– Anonymous

O kay, I just got back from seeing the movie *I Can Only Imagine* with a very dear friend of mine, and as I watched the movie a voice within said, "When are you going to stop dancing around and share your whole Truth?" So, let me just say this up front: my dad was an angry alcoholic and somewhat of a monster, and yet I cherished and loved him with every ounce of my being. Everything I did in my early years was for his approval.

I know I am not the first person who has experienced a family life like this, but I just so wish I would be the last. All I can do is share what my experience was – my Truth. I know that everything I am sharing is my very own perception, my world, my view only. I cannot speak for anyone else, not my siblings, not my parents, not anyone else in my family, even though we all lived under the same roof.

The point is that having witnessed what I did as a child caused a lot of damage in me. What I mean is that as I grew older, the choices I made in life were from emotional immaturity, enmeshment, longing to be loved, and a mega dose of major insecurities that led me to a life of drug use, drinking, and sexual expression that I won't even mention! With each decision I made, I was longing to be closer to my dad, the one I wanted to love me so badly, so longingly.

I do know today that my dad loved me. As much as I have changed and as much work as I have done on myself, I truly know and believe that. I don't willingly write this because I don't want to have to deal with family members; however, if I want to be real and stand in my Truth and accountability, you need to know where I am coming from. I don't live in the past anymore, but

I do share these perceptions of my memories with you so that you can understand why it is so important for me and such a passion of mine to help break the vicious cycle that continues every darn generation because we continue to choose not to change the life we may have made for ourselves.

I understand that there are those out there who don't know that they need to change or who are in so much pain, they have numbed themselves to the point that they can't get past the numbness. Believe me, I know what that feels like and what it feels like not to have any feeling at all other than pain.

My father never hit me, but I did witness him hitting my mother, often. What kind of messages does that send a child at six years old? What does it tell a little girl as she watches her knight in shining armor hurt someone he supposedly loves and had four children with? It was hell for me. My siblings and I each chose a different way to deal with it or not deal with it. I am in such awe of my siblings, having gone through what we did growing up and turning out to be some awesome individuals. For that I am truly grateful and love them with all of my heart. By no means am I saying that my father didn't love me – he did, I know it – however, the visions are always there, and the fear is always there, the memories of needing to hide in a closet or under my bed so I could silence the noise that went on outside my bedroom door.

When I was twelve, my parents divorced and my siblings and I lived with my mother. We moved back to the town where she grew up so that there was family around to help take care of us. Mom loved my father until the day she died, and I know that pain she carried was what caused her to drink. While living with her, things got a little tougher because she had to take care of her pain and wasn't always available for us.

My father then took us girls back to live with him after my brother graduated from high school. I was excited because I thought we were finally going to be in a safer place; however, my father passed out on the couch the first night back at his place and things went downhill from there. I lived with my father until I graduated from high school. By then, everyone else had left and, being the good caretaker I am, I couldn't leave. I was too afraid to leave him alone – I was sure he needed me. He didn't; he had his alcohol.

I moved to Austin after I graduated from high school and from there made some really big, poor choices. I was a late bloomer, never dated in high school, didn't drink, didn't go to parties, and chose to be a "good girl," too scared to do anything outside of my comfort zone, which was full of pain. I made up for a lot of that when I moved to Austin.

I was there for three years when one day there was a knock on my door and it was my mother with a U-Haul hooked up to her car. She said, "Get your stuff. You're coming home with me!" So I did. I found another dealer when I moved to where my mom was living; it took me a while to understand that all the numbing I was doing wasn't helping my situation at all. Like I said, I was a late bloomer.

At twenty-eight, I married a man I thought I loved, then later learned he didn't love me. I begged him to hit me – I knew I would leave him then – but he never would. He was so talented at mental, verbal, and emotional abuse. At the time those were not considered forms of abuse and no one ever talked about it. So, coming from the background I did, I believed everything this man said about me, and then some!

I finally woke up one morning and was done. I grabbed everything I could fit in my car and left. I drove to my sister's house, where my mom was at the time, and asked my mom if I could move in with her. The fear in me was so deep, I couldn't imagine being on my own at any point in time then. She generously said yes and I was back at home with my mom, feeling safe and sound – or so I thought.

My mother was my rock. She had lived through seventeen years of abuse, still loving my dad up to the day she died. I moved in, divorced my husband, and decided at that point in time, I would never marry again. I was done. Mom had been married and divorced twice and here I was going through a divorce. I had been told all my life how much I was like her and I knew I didn't want to experience that again, so as far as I was concerned, I was going to stay put where I was with my mom. We could grow old together, take care of each other, and know we would be together forever!

Well, evidently life had another plan. My mother died at the age of fifty-seven of lung cancer. I lost my mom, my best friend, and my home all at once. What the heck was I going to do now? My siblings and I sold her home; I moved into an apartment and began to live on my own for the very first time. Then one of my first miracles occurred.

It was 1991, my mother was gone, we had had to sell the house, and we had an estate sale after my siblings and

I kept what we wanted. The main thing I wanted to make sure happened was to donate my mother's best dresses to the women's shelter where I was volunteering at the time, in her memory. I dropped the dresses off so that the women there could have something nice to wear and never thought about it after that. I got my own apartment and hunkered down to a lot of loneliness and sorrow.

A friend started calling me once a week to ask me to come help her with a show they were doing at a little theater in a town close by. She wouldn't stop; she called for almost five weeks straight saying I could work behind the scenes, help create the costumes, work with the group, and get out of the apartment, on and on. I continued to tell her no, but she wouldn't let up. I finally caved in, went to the theater, and auditioned for a part. I had never done that before; however, I thought, "What the heck?" I got three parts, actually: a choirgirl, a reporter, and … a whore! Yep, you heard it right. The show was The Best Little Whorehouse in Texas.

My friend was right. The show kept me busy, with working full-time and rehearsal every week from Thursday to Sunday. The dress rehearsal came up and we were getting dressed in our costumes. I was in a room with about twenty other players, attempting to put on my "whore" makeup, when I caught something out of the corner of my eye. It was one of the other "ladies" putting on a dress for the scene when the cowboys dance with the ladies, and … it was one of my mother's dresses!

I asked her where the dress had come from. She told me they had found these dresses at a thrift store in Fort Worth, which is about twenty-four miles away from where I originally left the dresses at the shelter in Arlington. As I turned, there was another of my mother's dresses, and one more! She was all around me! No one knew how the dresses got where they did; however, they said to thank my mom for them. I informed them she had died three months prior and it got real quiet for a little bit.

When I went out on stage for that scene, I was smiling and crying at the same time. You see, my mom loved the theater. She even took it when she was in college. As for me, I got to dance with my mom one last time.

One of the things I realized when I began to wake up was that I was so judgmental. Now, I may not have said a word about it; however, the thoughts I had going on in my head were atrocious – so much so I was appalled by me! I realized this when I was at a Peace function with my husband in a room full of people from different religious backgrounds, cultures, and countries. As I assessed the room, I started hearing what I was thinking, and I was floored. I said something about it to my husband when we got home, and it really started bugging me. Who was I to judge anyone about anything? Just because I might not agree with their ways or how they dressed, looked, or their beliefs, I had no freaking right to say anything about anyone else when I couldn't even figure out what I was and how I wanted to show up!

I had been getting emails for a while from a group I had become interested in following, and one day a message showed up asking if I would be interested in being an interfaith minister. It hit me like a ton of bricks – that was it, that was it! I figured that if I could educate myself about others and learn more about their ways, I might be a lot less judgmental and a little bit more loving and compassionate. Lord knows, I sure could have used some of that!

After studying each religion, I truly know today without a doubt that we are all the same. We are so the same it is crazy! I no longer have to judge others, because I have learned through the studies of their ways that we are connected so deeply there is no way we aren't the same. Part of that learning was taking a look at myself first and listing the pros and cons of me. When I saw on paper how much I disliked myself, I got that I was putting that energy out on others and it was causing me to judge them in a way they weren't even being for the most part.

We are the same. Maybe not on the outside totally, but if we would take the time to sit down and talk with one another, especially someone we may not know – I know, scary, right? – it is amazing how connected you can feel with another, like you have known them forever. We are *so* the same!

Chapter 3

How to Solve What Has Been Holding Us Back

"Bring about restoration in your life in the areas that are holding you back!"
– Reverend Anne Tabor

When I first started going to church (oh, I left that part out earlier – my mother told me I could come live with her only if I started going to church. At the time I was desperate, so I told her, "I would do anything for room and board!"), I had no idea what I was doing. I just showed up. I sat in the very back of the sanctuary for the first six months I was there, crying. That is all I could do, just sit there and cry.

But I knew I was in the right place. Every Sunday, the talks that were shared were specifically what I needed to hear and yet I still didn't know what to do with the information I got. The bulletin one Sunday mentioned a group that met there at the church one night per week. After reading the description, I could honestly say I was the poster child for this group. At first I thought, "Wow, here is where I can start meeting some new people."

Well, little did I know that it was a group for ACOA (Adult Children of Alcoholics). The year I went to the group was one of the most painful in my life because I finally started to "wake up" to what was really going on in my life. I continued in this group for three years and then started in another Twelve-Step program and therapy, the two most important choices I made in the early stages of wanting to change my life and break this vicious cycle.

I stopped doing everything at once, and as the numbing wore off, the pain became so intense, I didn't know what to do with it. I was angry a lot: angry with my mother, angry with my father, angry with my ex-husband, and, most of all, angry with myself. There was a lot to work through at that time, and when you have nothing to stop the pain, you use whatever tools you have, whether they are healthy or not.

I hated myself for how I was behaving. I would hear the words that came out of my mouth and how I would talk to my mom or others I cared so much for, beat myself up for behaving the way I did, and then the cycle would start all over again. Thank goodness my mother and I had such a strong relationship and we were able to work through our stuff before she passed. I am so blessed by that.

I kept seeing myself as a horrible person until one day a number of months down the road a woman came up to me at church. We had been partners in a workshop we had taken together. She acknowledged me in a way I had never before heard from anyone about how much I had changed since she first met me, saying it was beautiful to be a witness to that. I so needed that validation at the time, and my eyes finally opened inside and out, which then allowed me to give myself full permission to become the person I truly wanted to be instead of losing myself in a world of fighting numbness and pain. It was difficult in the beginning because I didn't know what to do with all of these feelings and emotions.

Once I started working on me, going to workshops, and asking questions – lots of questions – with people I started to trust and look up to, I was able to really hear and connect with that tiny voice inside of me and to trust it fully. It took a lot of practice and a lot of mistakes, but I was directed in the right directions to help heal me, my inner self, and start looking at life in a whole different way.

When I started taking the steps I needed to work toward changing my life, I had no idea where to even begin. I knew that my life was not the way I wanted it to be; however, the only tools I had were the ones that got me to where I was and they were not healthy by any means. I was stuck. It is the most frustrating place to be. I knew I needed to change, I knew I needed to do something different, I knew that in my heart things needed to change, and yet I did not have a stinking clue as to what to do!

I started with therapy, and one of the biggest and hardest tools I used was mirror work, exercises where you look in the mirror, into your own eyes, and start telling yourself how much you love you. Yep, that is the biggest and hardest step ever. It was the most uncomfortable part of the work I ever have done. I was required to do the mirror work three times a day, every day. You look into your eyes and say, "I love you, [state your name]." Then you find affirmations that resonate with you and repeat them to yourself in the mirror daily.

Now, I'm not saying it is easy at any time, but I'll tell you this, once you get past the uncomfortableness of this exercise, you will become more willing to do other things that lead you in the right direction. If you feel uncomfortable doing this exercise, know you are on the right track. Until we are able to look into our own eyes and feel that connection of love for ourselves, it is difficult to cut through the other crap we have to deal with.

Chapter 4
The Part We Play

"When you are in a fix, often the fix is in you."
– Ashok Kallarakkal

I went to therapy knowing that the circumstances and situations I had going on in my life would continue until I learned some new skills and put them to work. One of the first skills I learned was journaling feelings, memories, situations, experiences, behaviors, and so forth. It was painful; however, it gave me information I didn't even know I had within me, information that had been buried so deep for so long that I didn't even know it existed.

One of the very first books I picked up was *Healing the Child Within*. I couldn't put it down until I read the whole thing. It was everything I had been feeling and everything I had been thinking. The most important piece was that it verified that I was normal after all. Then I started reading everything I could get my hands on; I was so hungry for more information to help me become the woman I am today. I was far from it and yet I knew that each book I read would lead me closer by showing me which exercises I needed to do, which workshops I needed to take, which people I needed to work with, and which connections I needed to make. It was so important for me to know as much as I could so that I could manifest what I really wanted to have in my life.

The books I read that helped me keep my sanity at this time were *You Can Heal Your Life* by Louise Hay, *Course in Miracles*, and anything by Wayne Dyer and Marianne Williamson. I was consumed with self-help back then. I believed we were the pioneers of the new thought and spiritual practices that are so valuable today.

Then there came the opportunities for workshops – "You and Money" by Maria Nemeth, "Coaching Certification" by Maria Nemeth, "Healing the Wounded

Child" by John Bradshaw. I created an accountability group with four women that ran for eight years and that met once a week so we could hold each other accountable in our baby steps. That group got us to where we are today. There also was a mastermind group – again, I created one at my home – and we met for five years, once a week, so that we could support each other in manifesting the life we wanted to have full of joy, love, and happiness.

It was always with trial and error; however, I learned very early in my process to listen to my instinct and to trust it beyond anything. Because of that, I was able to make very wise decisions that guided me in the direction I truly wanted to go. The biggest problem at the time was that I didn't know what direction I wanted to go in. I struggled for the longest time trying to make myself right and healthy. I was so focused on it that I wasn't able to see I was changing. No matter what tools and skills I had, I still would go back to my old behavior of beating myself up when I made a mistake. I would constantly berate myself and not understand when I was going to get things right.

I remember sitting in my mother's living room one night talking with her and starting to cry. I said, "I don't want to be fifty and not know what the heck I'm doing!" At the time I was thirty-one and still not sure where I was going. She came and kneeled down in front of me and said, "You are good now. Why can't you get that and that you are going to be just fine?"

She was right of course. Now, at sixty-one, my life is better than I could have ever imagined. Eventually, I began to understand that I was playing a part in all of this as well. The more aware I became of how I was reacting to situations in my life, the more I understood how my behavior had a big effect on how I reacted to each situation I participated in. When we finally decide that we are sick and tired of being sick and tired, we get the opportunity to examine ourselves. As we get stronger and have more knowledge about what is going on in our lives, we can then see what part we are playing.

Had I been healthier at the time I met my first husband, I probably never would have had anything to do with him because we would have been at totally different levels from each other. But because I was so down on myself, disappointed, depressed, and unhappy, I ended up attracting someone into my life who was just as messed up as I was. Of course, I couldn't even see that until I was willing to wake up and take a look at the situation from a whole different perspective. When we come from a family that doesn't know or teach their children healthy ways to deal with emotions and feelings or how to treat themselves and others with respect, we don't know there is any other way to deal with situations other than the way we were taught.

This point about understanding the part we are playing in our own lives is the most difficult one of all to grasp but also to explain. I had the hardest time trying to get that I was in the middle of all the problems I was having. I was so good at playing the victim role that every time I was told to look at myself and that I could fix my problems, I would get so pissed off and tell them they were full of crap. I could not for the life of me understand why I was to blame for being treated like crap.

This is still difficult for me to understand today, especially when family is involved, because there is that old behavior I fall back into so easily when it is someone I love so much. I let them push my buttons and so quickly I go back into the role I played in the family, it does not matter how old I am physically! The part that is most difficult for me today is finding the line between what part of the fault is mine and how much is the other person's, because it can be both.

The healthier I get, the less I take things personally and the less I am emotionally triggered. I also choose not to have certain people in my life because of the toxic dynamics they have. It is so very important to be aware and wake up to what part we are playing in this game called life! We can do so much more when the drama, stress, and anxiety are removed from our day-to-day stuff – and we are the only ones who can do that for ourselves. It isn't until then that we can wake up and take the responsibility to do the work we need to do so that we can be the light that so many others in this world need today.

Chapter 5
Changing Ourselves

"Be yourself; everyone else is already taken!"
– Oscar Wilde

We all long for connection and love. I believe these are the most important things in life that so many of us seem to be missing. We walk around daily not feeling we are good enough, well enough, or healthy enough, which then leads us to the need for numbing, which creates addictive behaviors – not just addiction to alcohol or drugs but also addiction to power, work, relationships, food, the internet, politics, anger, blame, victim roles, whatever. I spent more than half of my life playing the victim and being the martyr, sadly choosing to stay in my pain because it was my comfort zone and all I knew. Naively enough, I thought it was the safest place for me. I didn't know anything else, and I learned it from the best! I didn't know that I didn't know that I didn't even know that is how bad it was!

Then there was my dad, my knight in shining armor. No matter what he did to my mom or how he talked to me, I loved him more than life itself. Both of my parents loved me, there is no doubt in my mind, and yet I finally learned later in life that they were both doing the very best they could with what they knew to do. They weren't happy, obviously; however, I knew deep down inside that we children were very important to them and that they loved us the very best they could.

Now, that doesn't mean everything was peaches and cream. I was twenty-eight when my father died. I was young, naive, and ignorant, to say the least. I was living with my soon-to-be husband and my father wasn't thrilled about it. I called him one day, we got into an argument, and three days later he was dead. I never got closure with him the way I would have liked to, but I did get closure with him later down the road.

I have always known my father loved me; there was never any doubt about that. It was so confusing because of the behaviors that went on within our family, and yet I knew I was loved. It wasn't until I finally started becoming emotionally mature that I understood that my father wasn't a happy man and hadn't been for a very long time. It had nothing to do with me or any of us; again, everyone does the very best they can with the tools they have in that moment. It doesn't make what he did okay; however, it doesn't make him a bad person either.

Once we can see past the pain and feelings we had, we can then see everything from a whole different perspective. Because of that awesome awareness, my next miracle occurred. It was ten years later. In 1996, I was sponsoring the teens at our church along with my husband and we were invited to a rally at another church in Houston, Texas, where my father had lived before he died. I had not been back there since he passed because of the pain and anger I continued to hold onto since we never got closer.

I told my husband I would not be attending the rally and that he could take the kids on his own. He proceeded to share with me that we would be going to a large church in Houston, there would be a lot of support and love there, and because we were responsible for this group of teens our focus would be on them – I had nothing to worry about. After praying about it, thinking about it, and analyzing the crap out of it, I finally decided I would go. He was right, and what did I have to lose?

We arrived at the church, and as we came into the building, the congregants were offering their homes to us to stay in. Usually, it was one adult and at least six teens to a home. So when I was introduced to the couple I was to stay with, I asked them how many teens were going to be with us. Their response was, none. They were new to the church and wanted to be supportive but could only handle an adult – and I was it. Well, I got excited because I thought I was going to be able to have some downtime, at least at night, when I was at their home with no teens to look after.

I went to my husband, kissed him goodbye, told him I would see him the next day (this was before cell phones, believe it or not), and left. When I got into their car and we took off to go to their home, we started conversing and getting to know each other. I told them how kind it was of them to open their home, and they said they were glad they could do it; they had just moved into the place and were still kind of getting situated. As we continued toward their home, I got a very anxious feeling in my stomach and I couldn't for the life of me figure out why, until they pulled into the parking lot where they lived – it was my father's townhouse building! I kid you not, the same freakin' place my father lived before he passed. I sat in the back seat of their car in disbelief. When they opened their front door, theirs was the same layout as my father's place. The guest room I would be sleeping in would have been the same room I would have slept in had I been staying at my dad's. Ten years later. I say this with all my heart: if you don't deal with your stuff, it will find a way for you to deal with it!

The couple had no idea what happened in their guest room that night. I hid in the closet with a pillow stuffed in my mouth, sobbing and laughing at the same time. I looked like hell the next morning when I came out of there. My eyes were swollen, my nose all stopped up, and I still wasn't able to share with them what was going on. They took me to the church that morning and when my husband saw me, I started crying again. I told him what had happened and all he could say was, "Only you, Janet, only you!" Finally, I could let go of a weight I had carried around for what felt a lifetime.

What freedom comes from letting go of the past and allowing yourself to move forward into a life you have the opportunity to create the way you want it to be, not anyone else. I know that I am so different from the others in my family in that I am probably what is called "eclectic." I love bling, love bright, flashy clothing, and am such a people person – I don't know a stranger! I never knew that about myself until I was in my thirties.

It took a very dear friend of mine to give me permission to be okay with an outfit I was trying on one day when we were out shopping. It was nothing I would have bought myself. It was bright, multicolored, very tight-legged. I thought I looked like a clown. Along with that outfit, she picked out a pair of earrings, big chunky fish that were the same colors as the outfit. As I stood there looking at myself in the mirror saying, "No way could I wear this in public!" she said I wore it so well. She couldn't imagine it not being made just for me. It went with my personality.

It was a good thing I knew she loved me. For some reason that day pushed me into a whole different mind-set. She was right all along, and it was as if I gave myself permission to start being me when I purchased the outfit. I loved that outfit and it was the first piece that helped mold me into who I truly am. It started directing me into claiming myself, changing who I was into the person I always wanted to be. My clothing was the first thing that changed for me as I continued to change inside.

We spend the first half of our life wanting to be just like everyone else and not to stand out in any way, needing and wanting approval, love, and connection of some kind. Then we spend the next part of our lives attempting to find out who we really are and being that self no matter what anyone thinks.

Chapter 6

Past Situations that Made Us Who We Are Today

"Just be okay with who you are on your path."

It wasn't until certain situations like the ones I shared previously about my mom and dad that I realized that no matter what my past had been, it was my past. I made it through and now have the power and the potential to create whatever I want in my life. There are times when we may feel that we will never get past what is going on in our life; however, I have always come out on the other side of these situations a better person, more compassionate, with tons of empathy, knowledge, and wisdom I would have never known I had if I hadn't gone through what I had.

I love it when I witness individuals who stand in a grounded faith stronger than I have ever seen in my life. Some of them have had it way worse than I have and yet they believe with all their being that there is so much more to life than the situation that faces them and they also know that it is only temporary. Worrying is white-knuckling your way through life; letting go is making some room for the Universe to give you what you want. Not only are you going to grow spiritually, you will create some amazing things in your life that you may not even realize you can. Let go of the old to make room for the new.

I know today why I went through what I went through growing up and how very blessed I am because of it. Today I get to be who I am and do what I do because of my past experiences; I would never have gotten where I am today had the past not happened. At the time, you could have told me that and I would never have believed you, because I wasn't in a place where I could hear any of that. I fully understand today and know that I am able to work with my clients in coaching and ministry because I am able to understand those whose past has not been the healthiest.

I love working with individuals as they begin to see the light, when they begin to understand their own importance and see that they have so much to offer and that they have a purpose for being here. When we can look at our past and not react to it or allow emotions to control our lives, we have stepped up to our healing and we are growing mentally, emotionally, spiritually, and physically. When we are willing to look at ourselves and our behaviors and what part we play in the dynamics that we have created, we can assist others to do the same. By doing this, we then can help those who are so hurt that they truly believe the only way to get through their pain is with drugs, alcohol, suicide, hurting themselves, hurting their families, and even going so far as to use their weapons to hurt others they don't even know.

We are meant to be here for each other, and somewhere along the way we have lost that understanding. When we see others do a good deed, we call it a miracle or comment on how you never see people like this. I don't agree. There are so many good people out in the world doing amazing things, they just don't need it to be publicized, and at the same time our society feeds off of the negativity that is constantly shared on the news, on TV shows, in movies, and in video games.

I know today that because of my past, I can have empathy for others and not take it personally when they share their pain. I also know how to set boundaries and let people know that it is not okay to treat me the way they do, which is something I could never do prior to my healing. I can now thank my parents for the life they gave me. I am so blessed to have had a roof over my head, food on the table, parents who did love me, sisters and a brother who I love, and some wonderful memories as well.

My mother and father loved the theater, and when I was a kid and we lived in New York, we got to go to Radio City often and see shows there. My mom made all of us our Halloween costumes every year and, boy, was she creative! Every summer we would go visit my grandparents on my dad's side, and the cousins, aunts, and uncles, and go swimming at two water holes we loved, have picnics and BBQs, play games, fish, have fish fries, and connect with family. We went to the World Fair, baseball games, bowling, roller-skating, and ice skating … so many more wonderful memories. All of those memories, good and bad, make me who I am today – and I love who I am today! I am living a life I never in my wildest dreams could have imagined for myself. I am so blessed.

Chapter 7
Healing the Inner Child

*"We can't just acknowledge the things that we
saw as kids, we also must get in touch with
the feelings underlying those events so that we
can heal them."*
– Len Ellis

As I live today with my continuing longing to
grow, I still trust instinct and listen to where
it directs me. I tend to go in the direction
of therapy, hypnosis, tapping, gratitude journals,
affirmation lists, and, most of all, meditation. At one
point on my journey, I was blessed with the awareness
of wanting to become a minister. At the time, however,

I did not want to be a minister at a church but wanted to find a way to minister wherever I was, with whomever I was with. As I researched online what that might look like, I came across a website that offered online classes for interfaith ministers and I knew at that moment that was the direction I wanted to go.

It took four years of studying, homework, and tests online. After I completed learning about a religion, I was to go out into the community to find someone from that religion and have them teach me everything they knew. I was blessed to connect with a Buddhist temple here in my town, and I was even more blessed to meet the abbot at that temple, Luang Phi Payunsak, who is still my teacher today. Because of him and his guidance and teachings, I have had a consistent love for meditation since 2006. I was given a gift of flying to Bangkok and Chiang Mai, Thailand, to meditate with the monks in the temples in mountains for six weeks with no contact with the outside world. No phones, no computers, no talking with my husband.

Now, if you had told that young woman sitting in the back of the church in 1986 that she would one day be a minister and travel to Thailand on her own, she would have laughed and walked out of the building, never to return. At that time I was still carrying so much pain from my past, I couldn't see anything about my life ever improving because I couldn't see through all the pain. It took a lot of guts and courage to take the next steps and to be willing to look at those issues that I had not ever dealt with but that numbed my whole life. As I worked on those issues, it took everything I had to become willing to feel the pain that permeated my body and had been controlling my life all along. It was the hardest thing I have ever done – I seriously mean *ever* done in my life.

No one willingly wants to go to the places that are so painful or to revisit the most terrifying and scary parts in their life; however, until we do, we will forever be stuck. This is why most individuals choose to stay stuck where they are, because they think the pain of dealing with the past is so much more than they can handle. It may feel like it at the time, yet it's so very worth going through it.

I have lost so many people I love because they made a decision to continue to numb instead of to deal with their pain; most of them did not know that they had anything to work on. I continue to be surprised some days. Even now, I might be tooling along feeling like everything is wonderful and awesome, thinking things couldn't be better, but then my husband says something that triggers me, and I turn back into that wounded six-year-old wondering what I did so wrong, why no one loves me, and what the point is of going on.

Yes, there are times when I am done, I want to stop working on me, I don't want to do one more thing to improve myself – why the hell doesn't someone else do the work and stop telling me I am the one with the problem? Then I breathe, sometimes get help, sometimes just remember to use the tools I have, and once again move forward.

Once I made the choice to change and not live as the walking dead, there was no turning back. No matter what I feel some days, I will never go back to how it used to be for me, never, because I deserve so much more and the world deserves so much more of me. Again, it is the generational cycle that has to be stopped, broken, and discontinued so that we can open ourselves to each other in a loving way and let each other know that we are important and are here to make a difference in this huge, wondrous world.

Chapter 8

Knowing Your Passion

*"In time, you discover that you were
whole all along."*
– Deepak Chopra

When I was in my twenties, I knew deep down inside that I wanted to do something totally opposite from what I was doing with my life. I didn't have a clue what I wanted to do after I got out of high school other than that I did not want to ever go to school again, so college was out. That was when I packed up my stuff, left home, and moved to Austin. I moved there because my sister and brother were living there and I wanted to go somewhere where

I knew someone. I worked in a restaurant for a year and a half, then waitressed in a disco, and then bartended for a while. I moved to Arlington and started working in an office environment and continued to work as a secretary or administrative assistant because I fell for what I was told for so long: I wasn't smart enough to do anything more than that. I spent the next twenty-one years of my life closed up in a cubicle inputting data into a computer. Here I was, an extrovert who loved being around people, and I was in a cubicle! In 2000 I quit my corporate job without having anything planned. I just knew I had to get out of there or I was going to go crazy.

It was January, cold and rainy. I decided I needed to start yoga or do something to get me going and to get in shape and hopefully to give me the energy to figure out what I wanted to do. When I went to the yoga center, it was closed; however, there was a list of upcoming classes, and the first one I saw I immediately said, "Okay, God, I get it, this is a class I must take." I went home to call the facilitator to get information about the class and how much it cost.

As we talked, it was clear that this was something I needed to do; however, I was very hesitant because I had just quit my job and I wasn't prepared with any extra funds to do something outside of what I already was doing. The facilitator asked whether I was going to come, and I said I had to think about it. She asked if I hesitated because of the money. I said of course, and she said, so you need a scholarship? I asked what that meant. She said, just come.

I did a three-day intensive, and I never paid her. She gifted it to me, and it absolutely changed my life. From that day forward, I was able to define my passion, why I was here to make a difference in the world, and what work I had to do to become who I truly wanted to be. I first learned what my purpose was, and from that I was able to figure out what I wanted to do with my passion and what direction I wanted to go with it. I was so excited to be in this energy. I had never known how powerful I could be and that I really am here for a reason.

It is so sad when I witness and work with individuals who don't know what their passion is, don't know that they even have any because of what they have been told, been taught, or believed about themselves – and I totally get it, I was there! It also is amazing to see these people finally get that they are important enough to do the work with themselves to ignite that passion and move forward to what could be a mind-altering awareness that will change their lives forever.

People often say to me that they don't have any passion, they just want to do their job, make money, and take care of their families – which is good, but if they only knew that once they give themselves permission to touch their passion they will have an opportunity to change not just themselves but also their whole family in a very powerful and healthy way! My mission is to Ignite, Illuminate, and Encourage Authenticity in myself and others; I do that by creating a safe place for all who want to awaken to their full potential. I claim it, I know it, and I am now living it.

Chapter 9
Self-Care

"When you apply self-care to your real needs,
life becomes much lighter."
– Deepak Chopra

There comes a time in self-awareness when you have to really start taking care of yourself so that your old behaviors become a part of the past and don't continue to pop up unexpectedly and take control of your life again. When you come to the point of working on yourself and are aware behaviors are changing and interactions with others are more positive, you have to take a stand and claim your power fully and totally.

It isn't the easiest to do, even though it would seem somewhat simple. You can be pitiful or powerful – you cannot be both. For the longest time, I could tell I was changing and my life was becoming lighter and there was a definite light at the end of the tunnel; however, it didn't take any time for me to have a situation come up and within a matter of seconds I was back to the old behavior, reacting instead of responding, taking things personally and not understanding why I was still so messed up. I would forget how far I had come and only see where I was constantly messing up. I didn't need anyone else pointing it out to me or telling me how bad I was, because I was doing a great job of that myself – and there would be the vicious cycle kicking in once again.

Even though I was working on me, using the tools I had learned, reading the books, taking the workshops, I was not taking care of me fully. There is such a truth about the balance of a human being, as in the mental, the physical, the emotional, and the spiritual aspects. I was so focused on the mental, emotional, and spiritual, working on every aspect of those three; however, the physical was not my main focus. It was as if I had disconnected from my physical body in that whatever

I needed to do in that area was not my main focus. It is almost as if it is an out-of-body type of situation – what I mean is that being so focused on the other aspects of my life and being in my head so much, I totally ignored myself from the neck down. No exercise, no mindfulness when eating, and no focus on what types of food I was putting in my body. It was as if I was doing everything but living life fully in my body.

After my mom passed I really started taking a look at how I was treating my body and became very involved with holistic practitioners because it was about working on the "whole" of me. I worked with an iridologist and took supplements for many years and started eating healthier. Things were going great. I was feeling so much better, and my brain fog was gone. There wasn't any desire to touch any of the things I used to partake in to numb me, and that was huge! You see, when you are in the process of healing all aspects of your life and you are consumed with it, working so hard at getting healthier, sometimes you don't see beyond the hand in front of your face. I did not know that I had some physical stuff going on because I was so out of touch with my physical self while being involved with all the other healing going on.

So once again I was blessed with a healing; I don't know what year it was, but I do know it was shortly before the movie *The Green Mile* came out. I mention that because in that movie, one of the characters had the ability to heal others by pulling negative energy out of them and releasing it himself. Until I saw this movie, I wasn't able to describe what happened to me next. I was gifted another miraculous awareness in my healing process.

I was sponsoring our youth group at our church, as I had been for sixteen years, and another rally had arrived. It was close to home and we were looking forward to connecting with adults we hadn't seen in a while and taking new kids to the rally so they could experience the awesomeness of being one with their peers. Typically, it is a very consuming amount of time for sponsors because they have to stay two steps ahead of the teens to make sure everything runs as smoothly as possible. All of our time was spent taking care of the kids, and there was sleep deprivation and not a lot of downtime for us.

It just so happened that a very dear friend of mine, who was also a sponsor, had just completed courses on healing energy. We discussed how the schooling had been for him and what he might do with it next. I had been to my doctor the previous week with major female issues, and I was sent to a specialist who said that the only way to fix the situation was to have a full hysterectomy. I left the office in hysterics because I didn't want the surgery and I was still young and possibly wanted to have a kid one day. I told my doctor I wasn't going to do it, and she ordered tests for me to see how bad the situation was and then we would talk about it more.

I did the tests, left for the weekend, and thought nothing more about it. I mentioned to my friend that if he wanted a guinea pig to practice on with his healing touch, I would be glad to participate. Well, here it was, Friday evening at the rally, and for some reason we managed to have more sponsors than kids, so some of us did have free time available. My friend approached me and said that we could do some work, so we went to one of the cabins.

I lay down on a picnic table and closed my eyes. I don't know where I went, the only thing I do know is that at one point while he was working on me, he removed what I call a web of energy located right below my belly button and then he began to choke. My eyes flew open to see him turn and grab his throat as if he was choking. I didn't know what to do. There was another person in there with us, holding space. We just watched as he held his hand up to stop us and then he eventually settled down. At that point, for whatever reason, I felt something in me shift and I knew, really knew, that I was healed and would not have to have surgery at all.

That following Monday, I had to go back to the hospital to have a sonogram done, which would be the deciding factor in whether I had surgery or not. They did one sonogram and left the room to assess it, came back in and said they needed to do another one. They did and left the room again, leaving me there with a big smile on my face. They returned quite a few minutes later stating that there were absolutely no cysts and the issues that were occurring earlier were no longer occurring and I was free to go home – healthy, whole, and complete!

The biggest part of taking care of me is finding the balance in all aspects of my life, to be the whole being I want to be. That is always making sure that I am taking care of all of me, mentally, emotionally, physically, and spiritually. So many opportunities have come into my life since I chose to start taking care of me. I have been blessed to educate myself in a way that doesn't limit me to the basics that society believes are the only way, such as wanting a doctor to fix them with magic pills and make their pain go away.

Here again, you have to be willing to do the work that it takes to heal yourself physically as well as in all other aspects. I have chosen to do acupuncture, chiropractic, energy work, and holistic processes that have assisted in my health changing physically; however, I truly believe that one of the most important pieces of this puzzle is working your thoughts. Whatever is going on in our bodies and outside of our bodies is mostly coming from our thoughts. Everything that happens in our lives starts with a thought. Whether something is a positive or a negative experience, the thought came first.

Stop right now and just listen to what you are thinking. It is happening even while you are reading this. What are the first thoughts you had when you got quiet enough to hear them? Whatever you heard in this moment is what is running through your head behind the scenes. It was crazy when I stopped and allowed myself to listen to my thoughts for the first time. Unfortunately, they were so negative it was a wonder I functioned daily at all. I was blown away by what showed up for me, because on the outside, I am a pretty fun-loving, lighthearted individual, even freakin' funny! Well, there it was, on the outside – once I let someone get close, the sad, pathetic, pitiful me would then show up. I had no idea this is how I came across until I really listened to my thoughts and started to change them. It is so important that you understand this piece. Be willing to at least take a look at it for your own sanity. I know it saved me. There isn't any part of me that deserves any less and there isn't any part of me that doesn't deserve the highest and best for me.

Chapter 10
Practice, Practice, Practice

*"Renewal requires opening yourself up to new
ways of thinking and feeling."*
– Deborah Day

Again, as I said previously, you can be pitiful or powerful – you cannot be both. At this stage of your healing, it is so important that we have chosen the tools that work best for you now. They may change later in the process; however, you have enough tools to keep you moving forward, and at this time it calls for practice, practice, practice. It is time to let go of that baggage – until you do, there is no freedom. It is time to stop living in what was and move into what is;

crying over yesterday and living in the past – which is just our own perception – being offended, angry, or upset will only keep you stuck. You might be a product of your past, yet you do not have to be a prisoner of your past! You will have to put your foot down and say, "That's it. I may have gone through disappointments, I could have made mistakes, but I'm not going to waste the time I have left bitter over who hurt me, upset over what didn't work out. I am stepping out of the way and I am dropping the offense, I am dropping the guilt, dropping the failure, dropping the hurt, I am not living my life with any more baggage, I'm going to live my life free!"

Here is the key: if somebody hurt you, or if you made mistakes (and we all have), quit beating yourself up and know that you have done the very best that you were capable of doing at the time. If your mind is always on yesterday, that is the direction you will go. Calling people and telling them how badly you were treated all the time, constantly whining about how miserable your life is, and choosing to play the victim role – you're going to stay stuck. Now that you have an idea of which tools work best for you, instead of just talking about them, you have to actually start using them. This is where the saying "It is easy, but not simple" comes in.

In order for a behavior to change, it takes approximately twenty-one days of consistent focus on what you want to have change. As long as we continue to stay focused on the negative stuff, the whining, and the victimization, guess what it is you are going to get? One of the best practices for me still today is affirmations; once I choose the ones I am drawn to the most at a given time, I have multiple ways of practicing with them. I write them five times a day for twenty-one days, I write them out on sticky notes and plaster them all over the house, and I record them in my own voice and listen to them when I go to sleep at night. It is the only way that the old behavior can be gotten rid of and that the new behavior can take over. Along with affirmations, gratitude is a huge tool to be used daily to change your focus from the negative to the positive that you so long for in your life. I was born crossed-eyed and farsighted. At eighteen months old, I was wearing bifocals and diapers! I had to wear the cat glasses back in the late fifties and early sixties, the ones that everyone loves today. I wore the thick "coke-bottle glasses" all of my childhood and into early high school. My father got me contacts when I was in the eleventh grade. I had to wait for years because farsighted individuals didn't have the same options with eyewear as nearsighted people. The contacts got old quickly and I went back to glasses.

I was thirty-two years old, working diligently on new ideas and new tools, the biggest one at the time was affirmations. I looked at this one book every day, and I got an idea to record, in my own voice, all the affirmations in that book. It was the weirdest thing, listening to myself; however, I would play the recording at night while going to sleep and let it loop so that I heard it through the night and woke up to it in the morning as well. I continued to do this for about three months, not really thinking anything about it. It just felt good. I woke up one day and called my eye doctor because I knew it was time to get my prescription changed. I was having a difficult time reading clearly with my glasses, which happened occasionally for me, so it didn't seem like a big deal. At his office, he checked everything out, then turned and looked at me and said, "I don't know what the heck you have been doing, but you don't need your glasses anymore!" Once again, a change in my life I could have never imagined. I know that the healing work I had been doing with myself was finally showing up in a way where I could see the changes happening inside and out.

Chapter 11
Visioning the Life to Come

"What we focus on expands."
– Elizabeth Rider

It's not just about figuring out exactly what you desire; it's also about being grateful for what you already have. When you focus on what's already going right, stars align, miracles happen, and, suddenly, you have even more to be grateful for.

Four years after my mother was gone, and I was on my own, I decided that I was interested in possibly having another relationship, a healthy one. I worked on vision boards to find a healthy individual to be a part of my life. I made a list of everything I wanted in a relationship, covering all aspects in the man I wanted, not leaving anything out. I wrote out everything I could think of: looks, age, kids, money, healthy mentally, emotionally, physically, and spiritually – all the things that were important to me. I wanted to make sure that I covered everything and missed nothing. Eight pages on a legal pad later, I had covered it all, and then I took the list to the facilitator of my class, hoping to be shown how to bring a healthy man into my life.

The facilitator looked at my information, said what a good job I had done, and then said, "How much of this are you already?"

Well that was it; I was so mad, I took the papers out of her hands, tore them up, and walked out! The anger signaled the realization that she was right and that I still had work to do on me before I could find a healthy partner.

It took me a while to get over that one, I was so sure she was going to fix my situation without my having to do any work. How dare she make it about me! Linda Pendergrass was a mentor and someone who was very hard on you because she cared so much about you and wanted you to be able to see your worthiness, just as she did. I am forever in her debt and love her to the moon and back; sadly, she passed a few years ago and I long for her accountability and forwardness still today.

About three months after that, I sat down and rewrote a list, cut out pictures of the type of man I wanted, added a picture of me, created affirmations, wrote other comments, and included images of what type of life I could see and feel myself having one day in the near future. I set this vision board up in my bedroom so that I looked at it every day. Now, I am not saying that just looking at a board will give you everything you ever wanted; however, it is an effective exercise that can help you determine what you want. Feelings connect you to the images on the board so that you can believe them into your life.

I was single for four years, working at a company for three and a half years. This man had been working at the same company for about a year and a half. The company wasn't big; however, our paths never crossed until I was transferred from the marketing department to the engineering department. On that day, I was setting up my Betty Boop collection and this guy walked by and said, "Betty."

I said, "No, Janet!" … It then began.

We started dating, and after we were together for one and a half years, he proposed. When we were making wedding plans and finding a place to live, I was going through my stuff and came across my list and vision board. It had been a while since I had read the list, and to my surprise (I don't know why), everything I had put on that list, this man was. Amazing! We went to a workshop together before the wedding and we created vision boards for our wedding and our honeymoon: poolside in Austin at my sister and brother-in-law's home, with our honeymoon in Maui. The most loving and amazing experience ever, and here we are, twenty-five years later, me loving this man more than ever.

I tell every client I work with up front that vision board making is one of the top things we will do together, along with finding their passion and who they want to *be* in the world. Vision boarding doesn't mean you create a vision of what you want your life to look like, hang it on the wall, look at it as you pass by, and one day everything will show up out of nowhere. There is work to be done and most of all a connection to be made between believing and seeing what it is you want in your life and making it happen because you want it so much. What an amazing life!

Chapter 12
You Matter

*"The road to health for everyone is through
moderation, harmony, and a sound mind
in a sound body."*
– Jostein Gaarder

Now that you have an idea that there is a way you can create a life bigger, brighter, and amazingly more awesome than you could ever imagine, there are steps to take to do the work, knowing that every step you take and every choice you make guide you closer and closer to what you want. How exciting can that be? It is as if you have a clean slate and you can now create anything you want.

When you finally decide to know what your worth is and that you are here to make an amazing difference in the world, how would you not want to succeed and move forward in your life? There is a mantra that I use that is so important for me: "Surround yourself with those who celebrate you, not tolerate you." It is so important to create a support system for ourselves of people who want to see us succeed even more than we do and who will remind us who we truly are at times when we seem to have forgotten.

It is important to keep things in balance by using your tools of choice, asking for help, and loving yourself fully. You will always matter; you will always have a purpose that will direct you to the way your soul wants you to go. The most important thing you need to always remember is that you are loved. You are perfect just the way you are. No matter what faults you may have, they are part of what makes you who you are.

Right now … somebody is very proud of you. Somebody is thinking of you. Somebody is caring about you. Somebody misses you. Somebody wants to talk to you. Somebody wants to be with you. Somebody hopes you aren't in trouble. Somebody is thankful for the support you have provided. Somebody wants to hold your hand. Somebody hopes everything turns out all right. Somebody wants you to be happy. Somebody is celebrating your successes. Somebody wants to give you a gift. Somebody thinks that you *are* a gift. Somebody hopes that you're not too cold, or too hot. Somebody wants to hug you. Somebody loves you. Somebody admires your strength. Somebody is thinking of you and smiling. Somebody loves you for who you are … especially me.

I really believe that Marianne Williams has profoundly said it the best: "Our deepest fear is not that we are inadequate. Our deepest fear is that we are powerful beyond measure." It is our light, not our darkness, that most frightens us. We ask ourselves, Who am I to be brilliant, gorgeous, talented, and fabulous? Actually, who are you *not* to be? You are a child of God. Your playing small does not serve the world. There is nothing enlightened about shrinking so that other people won't feel insecure around you. We were born to make manifest the glory of God that is within us. It is not just in some of us; it is in everyone. And as we let our own Light shine, we unconsciously give other people permission to do the same. As we are liberated from our own fear, our presence automatically liberates others.

The work we have chosen to do is not just for ourselves. It is so important to wake up and start working on ourselves so that we can then assist others in waking up and seeing that we really are all one, longing for the same exact thing in life – to be loved.

About the Author

Janet Ellis is an impassioned speaker, life coach, and training consultant specializing in personal resilience, emotional and spiritual wellness, leadership, and organizational renewal for teens and adults. She facilitates a number of processes that guide teens and adults to become aware and acknowledge and claim their purpose in life, along with eight basic steps that will give them the power to follow their dreams.

Janet is a co-creator of the Teen Field Guide book *The Path* by Laurie Beth Jones.

Janet has inspired many groups and individuals to make positive changes in their lives. Through her company Janet's Planets of Empowerment, she designs and delivers inspirational workshops, seminars, and keynote presentations. Janet has been trained and licensed by Laurie Beth Jones to work as speaker, presenter, and facilitator. Ordained as an Interfaith Minister in 2006, Janet speaks and officiates weddings and funerals through different faiths and religious beliefs so that needs can be met in every way possible. This is one of her many ways to share and educate others that we are all one and working towards the same things, mainly being and feeling loved. Janet has extensive group leadership and counseling training from the Texas Association of Drug & Alcohol Counselors. She has training and experience in work style assessments, communication skills, behavioral intervention techniques, and time management skill building. She has served hundreds of individuals and organizations in business, non-profit, and faith-based sectors.

Thank You!

Thank you so much for taking the time to read my book. The fact that you were willing to read the book and you have gotten this far tells me something very important about you: you are hungry, searching, and ready to make some changes in your life. You are ready to wake up to Your Truth, ready to reach out and ask for assistance, and ready to break the cycle you have been habitually tied to until now! You're ready to experience your true life and what your purpose for being is.

I am here to support you in this process of change in your life, go to www.Janets-Planets.com, contact me, and together we will do an assessment to help you have a better understanding of where you have been, who you are today, and where you want to go for your future!